LAND
Ownership and Use

This book reviews the feudal system of land ownership which still pertains in Scotland, compares it with the situation abroad, and examines its effect on Highland land use and population. It initiates discussion on a number of topics — crofting most importantly, but also forestry, conservation, and access to the hills, which have to be reconciled when changes are eventually made. Finally it discusses systems of co-operative stewardship of the land which the authors believe would be conducive to developing the rural economy in Scotland's Highlands and Islands

ANDREW FLETCHER SOCIETY
1986

'Show me a man who loves all countries equally with his own, and I will show you a man who is entirely deficient in a sense of proportion. But show me a man who respects the rights of all countries, but is ready to defend his own against them all, and I will show you a man who is both nationalist and internationalist.'

'The Scots deserve no pity, if they voluntarily surrender their united and separate interests to the mercy of a united Parliament, where the English shall have so vast a majority.'

ANDREW FLETCHER OF SALTOUN.

Contents

Foreword

Land is the most basic natural resource. Its existence is essential to nationality, and the drive to possess it and defend it is as old as the Animal Kingdom itself. Its position on the Earth's crust, its relationship to the sea, its extent, the form it takes, and the material it is composed of, determine much of a nation's character and culture, and provide most of its resources. Husbanded properly, the land can yield a rich return *ad infinitum,* neglected, abused, or over-exploited, it can become a desert. Most important of all, land is finite. There can be no 'growth' in land, although in the past there has been plenty of growth in its value.

There are different levels of land 'ownership'. Every Scotsman, whether he is walking round the coast of Fife, or tramping the West Highland Way, or motoring through Deeside, feels that, in a way, the land of Scotland belongs to him, and increasingly he is demanding to be consulted about what happens to it. The tenant farmer, whether of a croft in Skye, or of a 600 acre farm in the Lothians, knows that in a real sense the land is his, and that some of the rights normally associated with the legal concept of ownership of property have passed to him. Then there are the legal 'owners', from the n'th generation crofter who has exercised his right to buy, to the Swiss business-man, purchaser of the Mar Lodge Estate, who climbed Ben Macdhui, and at the top asked his guide, 'Show me what I own'. Finally there are various public, community, and co-operative systems of land ownership. Perhaps, as is suggested in more than one of the papers in this book, the term 'ownership' is now redundant, and ought to be replaced by 'stewardship'. This term implies that obligations are involved, as well as privileges, when the ownership of land is considered. Moreover it is natural to conceive of different layers of 'stewardship', reflecting the actual situation, with matching privileges and obligations.

Land policy has been the Cinderella of Scotland's radical politicians, if not in words, then certainly in deeds. Of all the great issues affecting the people of Scotland, it has generated the most heat, but the least action. In two right-wing Tory parliaments, time has been spent changing or reversing previous legislation on almost every aspect of policy, except land ownership policy, for despite nearly 15 years of Labour rule since the Second World War, no significant legislation on rural land ownership was introduced. Indeed in 1978, at a time when there was galloping inflation in land values, when speculation was rife, and when overseas buyers had recently purchased 2 million of Scotland's 19 million acres, Hugh Brown, Labour's Scottish Undersecretary of State, said, referring to these matters, 'Of course we want the land to be owned by Scots, but we cannot be blind to the realities of the trading world we live in'. Far from being blind, the Scots are looking abroad, especially to Switzerland and Scandinavia, where they can see that land-ownership restrictions have encouraged thriving communities in unpromising circumstances.

Land ownership and land use are inextricably bound together, and the influence of one upon the other is referred to in several of the papers in this book. It is not possible to formulate policy on land ownership without considering the type of land, and the use or potential use of that land. Moreover it is likely that different forms of land-ownership (owner occupied, tenanted, community or co-operative ownership, or state ownership) may be appropriate for different areas, and certainly no blanket prescription is likely to serve the interests of the many different communities living in Scotland's diverse countryside.

In this book we have focussed mainly on the Highlands and

Islands where the history has been more turbulent and the problems are more acute. Furthermore in the freemarket system of land purchase in which Highland estates feature so prominently, and in the landlord/crofter relationship, we have customs and practices which are quite bizarre by continental standards.

The Andrew Fletcher Society has pursued its policy of seeking papers, not from politicians, nor from academics, but from those who are active in their particular 'field', with deep first hand experience of the problems about which they write, and who are galvanised by anger that so much of Scotland should be so exploited by people with such little involvement in the land that they (legally) own.

May, 1986   JOHN HULBERT (*Editor*)

The Law of The Land

By ROBIN CALLANDER

Landownership in Scotland is a property system that completely embraces the whole country: the 19 million acres (7.87 m.ha.) of land and inland water, the surrounding coastal waters and seabeds, all the airspace above these areas and also the ground below them down to the centre of the earth.

The laws of this system form the basis of the relationship between Scotland's two fundamental components as a country — people and place. It is through this system that the control and use of Scotland's land and other natural resources are determined. The purpose of this paper is to provide an overall perspective on this system of landownership, including the ways in which it might be improved.

Scotland's system of landownership is different from that in the rest of Britain because it is defined by Scots Law. The Scottish system is also unique in the modern world because the method by which land is owned is still legally classified as feudal.[1] (England, for comparison, abolished its feudal tenure in 1290). This indicates the antiquated character of many aspects of the Scottish system. It also points to the fact that the background to the issues of landownership and landuse in Scotland, is 900 years of feudalism.

THE PATTERN OF LANDOWNERSHIP

The simplest measurement of landownership in Scotland is the number of people who own land and the sizes of their properties. Scotland has the most concentrated pattern of private landownership in Europe, with the majority of the land held by a few large-scale landowners. For example, 60 per cent of Scotland's land area is owned by 1430 landowners (Scotland's population is 5.13 million). The pattern of estates amongst these main landowners is itself dominated by fewer and larger estates: 50 per cent of Scotland is held by 579 landowners, 40 per cent by 269, 30 per cent by 134, 20 per cent by 49 and 10 per cent by 13.[2]

These statistics mean that three-quarters of all privately owned land in Scotland is held in estates of 1000 acres (405 ha.) or more, half in estates of 5000 acres (2025 ha.) or more and a third in estates of 20,000 acres (8097 ha.) or more. For comparison, 100 years ago, when England was still considered dominated by large estates, less than seven per cent of its land was held in estates of 20,000 acres or more.

A prominent feature of Scotland's estate structure has been its relative constancy throughout its historical development. This dates back to the introduction of feudalism into Scotland during the 11th and 12th centuries. Precise figures are not available for much of this long history, but the trends are clear. The numbers of landowners increased up until the 17th century. In the 13th century, for example, when both the Crown and the Church had many and massive estates, estimates suggest about 2000 other landowners. By the early 17th century, when virtually all the former Crown and Church lands were in private ownership, the number of landowners was about 10,000, though only 1500 were major landowners. It was in the 17th century that the trend of the first five centuries of feudal landownership reversed and the overall number of landowners started to decline.

This new trend continued right through the 18th century and into the early 19th century, by which time the number of landowners in Scotland was down to about 7500. The fall was due to a reduction in the number of small landowners, with

the extent of Scotland held by the 1500 largest estates showing a marked increase. This incorporated the division of
Scotland's extensive commonties between neighbouring proprietors, while lochs which were not enclosed within a single
estate became the shared property of the surrounding landowners. These large estates maintained their position during
the 19th century. By the 1870s, 90 per cent of Scotland's
land was still owned by less than 1400 landowners, 50 per
cent by less than 120, 40 per cent by 63, 30 per cent by 34,
20 per cent by 21 and 10 per cent by 3.

Fig. 1 shows the change in these statistics by the 1970s.
The overall number of landowners had increased, but the
underlying pattern of estates remained remarkably constant.
For example, the change in the number of estates of 1000
acres or more between the 1870s and 1970s was only a
reduction from 1758 to 1723. The more significant change
was that the extent of Scotland held by these estates fell from
93 per cent to 63 per cent. This reduction is nearly entirely
accounted for by the growth of state owned land during this
period from 0.2 to nearly 13 per cent of Scotland and the
spread of owner occupied farms to cover approximately
another 11 per cent of Scotland. Scotland has the smallest
proportion of owner-occupied farms in Britain, but has a
higher proportion of state owned land. The Forestry Commission and Department of Agriculture and Fisheries account
for over 75 per cent of state owned land, with the rest held by
other government departments and agencies, the Crown
Commissioners, nationalised industries and local authorities.
Between the 1870s and 1970s, urbanisation accounted for
another 1.5 per cent of Scotland, but had little effect on estate
structure. Over 97 per cent of Scotland is still rural land.

The ownership of Scotland's estates shows, like the estate
structure, a relatively high degree of continuity from past
centuries. There have always been new entries to the ranks of
Scotland's landowning families, from the original anglo-

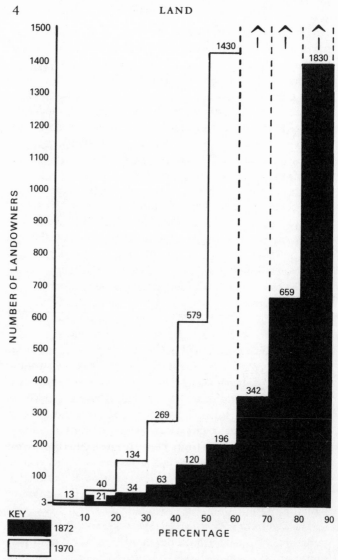

FIG I.   The percentage of Scotland held by the largest landowners, 1872 and 1970.

normans to today's foreign buyers. However, since the anglo-normans, the different types of incomers during each century have never acquired more than a relatively small percentage of Scotland. Thus, although all the phases of Scottish land-ownership are represented amongst the present estate owners, it is estimated that, for example, 25 per cent of all estates of 1000 acres or more have been with the same families for over 400 years. These include families that have been the heredi-tary occupiers of the same land for more than 30 generations since the arrival of feudalism and a particular predominance of families from around the 13th century. Over and above this 25 per cent, are those families that have held their present estates for less than 400 years, but can trace their landowning ancestry back to the 16th century or earlier.

Both the pattern of Scotland's large estates and the compo-sition of the group of people who own them owe more to events many centuries ago than to any recent influences or requirements.

THE POWER BEHIND THE PATTERN

The ownership of land in Scotland has always granted wide-ranging rights over that land to the owner. These rights have conferred political, social and economic advantages on their holders and provided the power behind the persistent pattern of landownership in Scotland.

Landowners have always sought to maintain and strengthen their control over their land. Their success at this during the historical development of feudal landownership in Scotland, is reflected in the authoritative 19th century observation that 'In no country in Europe are the rights of the proprietors so well defined and so carefully protected'.[3]

Legislation was employed to protect the land for those that held it. For example, the laws of entail could be used to ensure that estates would not be broken up in the event of bankruptcy or other misfortunes. At the same time, the law was developed to complete the landowners' monopoly over the resources of their land. Sporting rights provide an example of this. When feudalism became established, there was no relationship between sport and landownership. Any free person could hunt any wild animal where he wanted and the game belonged to whoever killed or captured it, regardless of where he did this. However over the centuries and culminating in an act of 1621, sport was converted into an exclusive right of property. This could not be achieved by claiming ownership over the wild animals, but was established by making landowners the only people who could hunt on their land. This is still the legal position today.

However, despite the power of landownership, the control that landowners have over their land is relative. Landowners in Scotland can use their land as they please, subject to the constraints of their feudal title to the land, statutes and common law. The title or authority by which landowners own their land is derived from the highest authority in Scotland. In legal theory this is God, but in practice it is the Crown, who is the ultimate owner of all of Scotland and is known as the Paramount Superior.

Any landowner is thus a vassal of the Crown. The essential character of Scotland's feudal tenure is that this need not be a direct relationship. Anyone, when he disposes of land he owns, can maintain an interest in that land. He, as a vassal to the Crown, is then the superior of the new owner, who becomes his vassal. There is no limit in Scots law to the number of times this process, known as subinfeudation, can be repeated over the same piece of ground. At each stage, the superiors can limit the extent of possession conveyed by reserving rights to themselves and by imposing additional conditions and burdens on the vassals. There is no ceiling to these limitations and this adds to the immense complexity of the long chains of superior-vassal relationships.

The pattern of landownership in Scotland is thus not as

simple as the map provided by estate boundaries. For example, estates that have contracted to a small size, may have retained the mineral rights over the whole of their former extent. They could also have stipulated that, for example, all the buildings on their former estate lands have to be maintained with a certain colour of paint-work. The rights retained by superiors create 'hidden' maps of landownership which, with an example like minerals, are even more concentrated than the pattern of estates.

The other main constraint on the rights of landowners are statutes. Considering sporting rights as the example again, Acts of Parliament have steadily shortened the list of species which landowners can kill, progressively reduced the choice of methods they can employ and the length of hunting seasons available to them. While some species survived outside the landowners' monopoly as 'vermin', some rights over other species have been given to other people in special circumstances. For example, the Acts from 1880 onwards allowed agricultural tenants to deal with rabbits, hares and deer that are causing serious crop damage.

Legislation continues to accumulate on many aspects of rural landuse and settlement. These statutes can be construed as an erosion of property rights to the extent that they regulate the powers of landowners over their land and the people living on it. However, by virtue of being restrictions, they have not tended to create opportunities. All the main rural resources including those for agriculture, forestry, sport, recreation, natural conservation, quarrying, settlement and development, remain controlled within the same pattern of landownership.

THE POTENTIAL FOR LAND REFORM

Rural Development is needed to meet the aspirations of rural communities and of society at large for its rural environment.

Landownership is the central institution in rural Scotland, because it controls natural resource use. Rural Development will therefore either rely on property rights or be confronted by them.

Successful Rural Development needs to be based on local resource use under local control. The United Nations and other development agencies have long recognised that the pattern of landownership can be the major obstacle to this. The World Bank, for example, would not give development grants to Scotland without a major reduction in the extent to which the land is held in so few and so large estates.

An increase in the number of landowners is a prerequisite for successful Rural Development in Scotland. The simplest method of achieving this is a redistribution of land based on upper size limits of ownership related to land quality. There are many recent examples worldwide of how different countries have arranged this. However, the experience of all these examples is that a redistribution of acres is inadequate by itself. For example, all landuse and related rural policies, including the support systems relating to grants, marketing, and advisory and other services, will all be geared to the old pattern of landownership. Any redistribution of land will have to be a comprehensive package, normally labelled Land Reform.

An essential requirement for any redistribution is a register of land or cadastral, giving details of ownership, quality and use. Scotland is very unusual amongst European countries in not already having a cadastral and the complexity of Scotland's feudal tenure makes the compilation of one particularly difficult. However, the abolition of superiorities, which has been suggested by several law commissions since the beginning of this century, would simplify this. The abolition presents no particular problems and would not alter the extent of land held by owners. It would, however, have a redistributive effect, as the rights of superiorities tend to be held by the larger estates over smaller landowners.

These steps can be related to two other aspects of reform. Firstly, it would bring Scotland in line with most countries by excluding foreign nationals from landownership in Scotland. Eligibility for ownership could also be related to residence requirements, as has been the case in relation to various property rights in Scotland in the past. Secondly, it would redefine the existing law on the range of impersonal or legal arrangements (e.g. partnerships) that can be employed to own land in Scotland.

The abolition of feudal superiorities requires the removal of the Paramount Superior. This could involve transferring the inalienable and ultimate ownership of all of Scotland to a more democratic concept, such as Scotland's traditional 'Community of the Realm'. At present, the Crown also holds various property rights directly and others in trust for the public (eg. coastal waters and rights of navigation). Some of these might be strengthened (eg. access) and all could be held in trust through the authority of parliament.

During this century, the Crown has reclaimed rights (eg. coal) and reserved others to itself (eg. oil and gas). Its successor could extend this process, by for example, reserving high altitude land and irreplaceable nature conservation sites. These would be held in perpetual public trust, even if granted back to local management. The Crown's successor could also delegate or grant out some of its rights to the regions and beyond (eg. minerals, coastal waters). The redistribution of such important resources is a strategic requirement of Rural Development. Each area will need a strong degree of control over its own natural resources if it is to be able to counter centralisation − the antithesis of Rural Development.

In organising landownership below the level of the Ultimate Owner, a balance also needs to be reached between personal and public or communual rights. Two of the lessons from Scotland's feudal experience are that the control of rights can be held at several levels simultaneously and that different rights can be held by separate parties over the same area. Such pluralism would also need to be a feature of a modernised system. Redistributing land and land-based rights to increase the opportunities for Rural Development could involve many options over, for example, rivers and inland water and also sporting and mineral rights. As with large areas of uplands, control by the local community can be compatible with individual use. This redistribution should affect both private and state lands and rights.

At the same time as any redistribution, there is the opportunity to remove the contradictions that have built up between feudal ownership and statutes. Such a new definition of property rights can also incorporate the further limits to acceptable landuse practices that may accompany land reform. The term 'ownership' may itself, as some legal authorities have suggested, be considered redundant. With a hierarchy of titles and mass of statutes, it is already a very relative term and will only be more so in any new system, where concepts akin to trusteeship or stewardship are more closely defined.

Land reform will need to incorporate many attributes if it is to be viable and satisfactory in the short term, as well as resilient and capable of sustained improvement in the longer term. As the basis of Rural Development, the challenge should not be underestimated. Rural Scotland has a long history of decline, the fate of its communities contrasting sharply with the continuity in the pattern of landownership. The spiral of decline continues, with present public policy trying to buffer the trend with subsidies. Land reform and Rural Development will require investment, but towards a more self-sustaining and healthy rural sector. That sector would use its own resources to offer creative opportunities to those that live there and to those that wish to join them, while also enriching Scottish society at large.

There is little hope for rural Scotland without an integrated scheme of land reform. It may be approached in gradual stages or in a smaller number of more major changes. For too long, the land of Scotland has been subject to one ruling idea, developed as legal theory and expressed as law. Scotland's feudal system has been the Law of the Land for nine centuries. The future can not rely on just altering and adjusting aspects of this ancient system. The ideas and values of Rural Development represent a different theory of the relationship between people and place. The future lies with a modern Scottish system that rewrites the Law of the Land.

NOTES

1. There are two small exceptions to this. Firstly, alloidal tenure, which principally involves lands held directly by the Crown and Church and which is an integral component of the feudal system. Secondly, udal tenure, the remnants of which survive in the Northern Isles and which is the only genuine exception to Scotland's feudalism.

2. The dateline for the modern statistics is 1970. No overall statistics are available for any more recent dates. However, there has been no significant change in the general pattern since 1970. The sources of all the statistics are given in my forthcoming publication 'A Pattern of Land-ownership in Scotland'.

3. Sir John Sinclair, 1814.

Scottish Land-holding and its Social and Cultural Aspects compared with Swiss and Scandinavian

By ADAM WATSON and
R. DRENNAN WATSON

Scots are so used to Scotland's past and present land-holding that many think there is nothing unusual about it. In fact, it is very unusual for continental Europe and north America, as you can check by asking people from there. When making comparisons with elsewhere, it is useful to look at land-holding from scratch, in an objective way that is free from party political preconceptions. It is also useful to consider land-holding and landuse not in isolation, but as an inseparable part of a community's well-being and culture.

In this chapter we do this for Scotland compared with Switzerland. What we write comes largely from our report in 1983, printed by Grampian Regional Council, following a study tour in Switzerland. We also refer briefly to Norway and Sweden, using publications and also our own experience there.

A comparison with Switzerland is of great value for Scotland. A small country with much poor mountainous land, a largely urban population of 6½ million, a high standard of living, and extremely low unemployment, Switzerland clearly deserves careful study by people concerned about Scotland's problems.

The Swiss have developed one of the longest and most vigorous democratic traditions in Europe. A Community is the most basic level of government, usually consisting of a village or group of villages, and the neighbouring countryside. The population varies in different Communities from 500 to several thousand. Community Councils have the main powers over planning control of development (Gilg 1985), and can raise money by taxation. Instead of abolishing small councils and centralising power, as we did with local government reorganisation in the 1970s, the Swiss have held on to a far greater devolution of power than we ever had.

A much larger proportion of the land's resources is under local community control than in Scotland. Much of the alpine pasture is communal or owned by cooperatives involving a number of individuals or families grouped together. About two thirds of the forests are owned by various public bodies such as Communities, or by 'Citizenships', the local political organisations that existed before the Communities. The emphasis is on local communal or cooperative control, not state control. Large state organisations are not important landholders.

Most houses are owned privately by their occupiers, and likewise most farm houses, farm buildings, and arable farmland. It is possible for an individual Swiss to own a larger area, but this would incur larger compulsory pledges such as repairs to roads and streams, by order of the local Community Council. In practice, big estates owned by private individuals or private institutions are not a feature of Switzerland. In past centuries, aristocratic families did have large land-holdings. The families still exist but have no more direct power over land than anyone else. Nowadays they provide an important public service in the law, politics and other professions.

A foreigner is generally allowed to own land, mostly in the form of a house and garden. Only recently were fairly weak legal restrictions on such foreign landownership introduced, but an effort is now being made in the Federal Parliament to ban the sale of further land to foreigners.

Dutch, Swiss, Norwegians, and other foreigners have bought large Scottish estates since 1960, and some have made big profits by selling land. These people do not own similar large estates in their home countries, and a Scot would find it very difficult or impossible to be a big laird in Switzerland or Norway. This illustrates how one-sided our arrangements for land-holding and selling are in Scotland.

Switzerland has only 8 per cent of its population in farming, about 80,000 families in all, and mostly all small farmers. The largest farm covers only 360 hectares, and this is regarded as quite exceptional. The average farmer in the mountains has only ten to twenty cows. This farming has high labour costs and low productivity, and cannot compete in the open market with food from intensive lowland farming. For this and other reasons there has been a drift from the land, as in many other parts of the Alps. For various reasons the Swiss have been anxious to prevent this (Popp 1978). Far more than in Britain, they feel that their culture, and the values that they wish to preserve, are tied up with the upland rural communities and their life style.

Three industries – agriculture, forestry and tourism — dominate the Swiss alpine countryside. None alone, and no two together, can now support an adequate population to maintain many rural communities at a viable size. Although some cases of tourist over-development have occurred, generally the three industries are better integrated than in Scotland. Many individuals get a living from all three, working partly in agriculture, partly in forestry, and partly getting money from services to tourists.

The inter-dependence of all three is clearly realised. They can either be mutually supporting, or one can destroy the others if it becomes too dominant. Further, a decline in any one of them has serious implications for the viability of the other two. All attempts to stop rural depopulation by establishing large-scale industry in the uplands have failed unless based on some local resource such as granite quarrying. Hence the integration of these three industries is central to Swiss rural landuse policy. In contrast we subsidise agriculture and forestry in ways that are often harmful to tourism.

One sharp contrast with the Scottish Highlands is the large, thriving communities in the Swiss mountain valleys. Although there are some villages in very high or remote valleys which are partly or wholly deserted, most villages are thriving. Many people are living in high villages in very difficult terrain. The key importance of services such as public roads, small local hospitals and schools is strongly realised. For example, in the mountainous Canton of Graubünden a school is not closed unless the number of pupils falls below eight, a much lower number than here.

Switzerland became a world leader in tourism very early. Tourists came to see the mountains and the attractive valleys with their mixture of forest, farmland and traditional villages, and enjoyed the good service in hotels. The famous resorts have increased in population due mainly to immigration from other parts of Switzerland and by temporary foreign workers. However, rural areas which depend on agriculture and forestry have had greater population stability, with no big drops or big increases (Council of Europe 1973). Areas relying mainly on tourism have had large population declines during periods of world stress, such as during the second world war. The current world recession is another example where resident numbers have begun to decline in tourist areas again.

Tourism is important in maintaining a high standard of living in rural communities, but in some places in Switzerland it has over-developed and become damaging to the local community as well as to itself (Kommission, 1979, Krippendorf 1982). On the other hand, mountain communities which have not been able to boost their income by tourism tend to be relatively poor. The Swiss have an interesting way of twinning rich and poor communities. The main aim was to aid the transfer of funds from rich to poor communitites. However, a major extra benefit has been that disparate communities have developed a better understanding of each other's problems.

Because of the much greater devolution of power than in Scotland, Swiss local communities have much greater scope to take their own decisions and influence their own destiny. Local individuals and groups retain ownership and control over a much larger proportion of their own local resources, including land, forests and farms. The local language, dialect, traditions and architecture are still largely intact, as is the local population itself and its pride in these things. This sense of identity and cultural pride is important in encouraging local initiative.

The Swiss put much importance on sustaining not just local populations, but their indigenous cultures and traditions as well. Initiative from within the community is regarded as a vital part of any development plan, without which outside aid tends to founder. This initiative depends largely on the local community's self-confidence. This in turn depends on how strongly the community believes in its own values, traditions, language and dialect, and how well it feels that others hold these in esteem. There is a glaring contrast here with the fate of our Gaelic and Lowland Scots cultures and communities.

It would be misleading to claim that these social and cultural aspects of land-holding are the sole reason for the relatively thriving communities in the Alps. Farmers in the Alps have a warmer summer and usually better soils than our high farms. Obviously this helps, but the land-holding and cultural pattern that we have outlined is of more importance. This can be seen if one moves north to parts of Scandinavia which have poor soils and a worse climate than Scotland, but yet where the rural communities are thriving.

Scandinavian farmers are subsidised, as are Swiss and Scottish ones. But an important difference is that most of our small farmers are still not owner-occupiers. Also, Highland crofters had no security of tenure until the Crofters Act of 1886. Our tenant farming families lacked it until the series of Agricultural Holdings Acts which began in 1883 and were made substantially stronger in 1948. (Later legislation was a setback to tenants; as recently as the 1960s, a tenant was not entitled to pass the tenancy to his offspring, and this was redressed only by further legislation, which still holds today.) Laing (1837) compared our crofters and their Norwegian counterparts. Although the latter had worse terrain and climate than in the north-west Highlands, their ownership of the land and the benefit that came from receiving 'the advantage of their own exertions' had led to better tended farms and better houses. In Norway were to be found 'the Highland glens without the Highland lairds.'

On treeless coastal parts of north and west Norway, most farmers are part fishermen. Like Switzerland but unlike Scotland, most farmers in forested countryside in Norway are part foresters, owning some woodland, and local communities control much of the forest and the alpine pasture. Many farmers in Norway get substantial extra income from tourism, as in Switzerland.

Swedish landuse and land tenure also provide a contrast to the Scottish Highlands and uplands. About 60 per cent of Swedish farms are owner-occupied. The forestry pattern differs even more markedly from Scotland. About one quarter of Swedish forested land is publicly owned, mostly by the state but also much by municipalities, the church, and other public bodies. About a quarter is owned by private forestry companies, and about half is in private ownership. Private ownership is predominant in southern Sweden, where it is spread among 240,000 private holdings. In half of these, the forestry is worked in conjunction with agriculture, showing the importance of agro-forestry in Sweden. In fact, in southern Sweden, farmers manage about two thirds of the forested land. It is also of interest that, as in Norway and Finland too, Sweden has an 'everyman's right' on access to the countryside, so that people can walk or ski freely in woods, meadows and open hill country.

Scottish forestry in recent decades provides a marked contrast with Switzerland and Scandinavia. In Scotland, there was at first a big expansion by a large state body, the Foresty Commission, and some expansion by private estates. In the last two decades the main expansion has involved a few large private companies. In both these monolithic cases, local people have gained little, apart from a small number of relatively subordinate jobs, and above all they have no control.

In recent centuries, Scottish landuse has had a history of domination by large private estates, over nearly all of the Highlands and substantial parts of the other uplands and the lowlands. Recent decades have seen more owner-occupiers of farmland on lowland and strath, but private estates still dominate landuse over much of Scotland. In addition there is now a very large land-holding by state bodies (the Forestry Commission, Department of Agriculture & Fisheries for Scotland, and to a lesser extent the Nature Conservancy Council and Ministry of Defence). Furthermore, increasingly extensive areas of Scottish farmland and hill ground are owned by large institutions such as insurance companies, pension fund companies and forestry companies, whose managers and headquarters are nearly always more remote and anonymous than the private lairds whom they have supplanted.

Partly because of this long-term domination of landholding and landuse by people usually outside the local vernacular community, general knowledge about landuse practices and planning, and participation in them, have been largely lost from the local population in Scotland, but not in Swiss and Scandinavian communities. Scottish local authorities do little to educate people in landuse. Understanding is an essential prerequisite for participation. It would help if school children were given more education in the language, tradition, social history, land-holding and landuse of their own neighbourhood. These are virtually untreated at primary school and scarcely touched upon at secondary school. Children may study history and geography, yet remain ignorant of their own cultural and landuse background. Hence they are more likely to turn their backs on the community by emigrating.

The best thing that could happen to our rural individuals and communities is that they become more self confident and move towards being in greater control of their own destinies. That, and not just handouts of money from outside, is the main lesson that Swiss and Scandinavian experience can offer to Scotland.

REFERENCES

COUNCIL OF EUROPE (1973). *Economic and social problems of mountain regions.* Study Series Local and Regional Authorities in Europe, no. 5, Strasbourg.

GILG, A. W. (1985). *Landuse planning in Switzerland.* Town Planning Review 56, 315-338.

KOMMISSION (1979). *Das Schweizerische Tourismus-konzept.* Grundlagen für die Tourismuspolitik Schlussbericht. Beratende Kommission für Fremdenverkehr des Bundesrates. Bern.

KRIPPENDORF, J. (1982). *Fehlentwicklungen im Schweizer Tourismus.* Schweizerischer Fremdenverkehrsverband SFV, Bern.

LAING, S. (1837). *Journal of a Residence in Norway.* Second edition, London.

POPP H.W. (1978). *Swiss experience in policy for upland areas.* The Future of Upland Britain (Ed. by R. B. Tranter), pp. 659-668. Centre for Agricultural Strategy, University of Reading.

WATSON, A. and WATSON R. D. (1983). *Tourism, land use and rural communities in mountain areas: the Swiss approach and its relevance for Scotland.* Report available at Grampian Regional Council, Woodhill House, Aberdeen.

The Role of Conservation in Highland Landuse

By FRANK RENNIE

There is little doubt that the Agricultural Industry in Europe is at a turning point, and that the road which lies before us represents a new socio-economic direction into future European attitudes towards land management and landownership. Whether we like it or not, the political judgements surrounding this issue concern every one of us, either as consumers or producers, so it is as well for us to try to obtain a crystal-clear picture of the available options. It has been said that at the present time there is nowhere in Europe which could be worse for the small farmer than within the UK. It has also been said (almost, but not quite, in the same breath), that there is nowhere in Europe better than the UK for the future presented to big farmers. It follows from this that the gap between small and large farmers in the UK is the greatest such gap in Europe, and we could reasonably expect the gap to be even greater in Scotland. This is because the Highlands and Islands which comprise nearly 50 per cent of the land area of Scotland, is mostly poor quality land, suitable at best only for 'marginal' upland farming.

It has long been apparent that the policies and grant-incentives which spring from each of the various departments of the British Government concerned with landuse are often in direct contradiction. Competition for the use of the land between agriculture and forestry, or between either of these activities and the encroachment of the ever-increasing urban sprawl has become commonplace. It is this very growth of the

20

cities which has led to the relatively recent realisation of yet another major type of landuse, that of the conservation of the natural environment. It seems that the more the majority of the population are cooped-up in the cities, the more they want to take-off to the hills at every spare opportunity, and consequently the more pressure is applied to the remaining countryside to be 'a lung of the city'. The question is whether rural areas should simply be a weekend playground for the towns, or a place to live and to earn a decent living for the rural inhabitants themselves? Can both of these needs exist side-by-side? Moreover, as farming intensifies its activities in response to Government incentives, and as more people demand access to the countryside, these very areas and their features of landscape, wildlife, and unspoilt 'naturalness' which are being sought after, are being destroyed.

The official response to this (largely stemming from greater public awareness and the rise of popular and effective environmental pressure groups), has been the notification by the Nature Conservancy Council of selected areas as National Nature Reserves, and more widely of Sites of Special Scientific Interest (SSSI). These latter areas may extend from a fraction of an acre to several thousand acres, and are designed to ensure the protection from damage (accidental or intentional) of areas of National importance for wild plants and/or animals by outlawing certain practices which may destroy the importance of the site, and by restricting other potentially damaging activities until subject to approval by the NCC. It is sad that such restrictive action is necessary to protect these areas, and it is probably true that both conservationists and other landusers regard the situation as being far from ideal.

Both are right of course. What we need is a much more responsive system of land management where conservation takes an equal position with agriculture, forestry etc. in the pattern of rural landuse and (most importantly), in the rural economy. I believe much can be learned by looking in more detail at the crofting system to see how the needs of conservation of the natural environment can be effectively integrated into the needs of the rural community. The crofting communities can provide a most efficient springboard for a radical shift of perspective in treating conservation as a type of landuse which can benefit the direct landuser (in the crofting counties), and the indirect landuser (in the urban areas).

The recent changes of emphasis in the European scene away from intensive agricultural (over)production and towards agricultural systems which are 'environmentally beneficient' places the crofting communities in the forefront of the new movement. The crofting system is and always has been much more than simply a method of small scale agriculture; it is a complex social system in which the availability of land, and the attachment to the land allows communities to survive, and even thrive in otherwise very adverse conditions.

To see that this is true we need only compare the population density of a crofting area such as Lewis or Uist with the emptied glens of many west coast mainland estates. The facts that crofts are so small in comparison with even small mainland farms, and are on such poor ground have meant that crofters have necessarily diversified their sources of income to more than that which can be gained by agriculture alone. Most crofts are classed as spare-time activities, and many are part-time. In fact the full-time crofter has the worst of both worlds, neither big enough to compete effectively with the mainland 'free markets' which are increasingly profit orientated and geared towards the larger units, nor having the benefit of an alternative source of income to tide him through the more difficult times. The small-scale, low-input, low-output highly diverse style of crofting landuse, and the wide range of other occupations undertaken by crofters, have ensured the maintenance of reasonably healthy and viable rural communities, and led to the development of an intricate patch-work pattern of landuse in a relatively small geographic area. This in turn provides a great variety of different habitats for wildlife.

It is too easy to scoff at crofting as being a rather primitive form of agriculture because of its small-scale, traditional nature without giving due credit to the much more positive contributions of the crofting system towards integrated rural development. The time has come, I believe, for the conservation movement as a whole to reinforce this system by the creation of conservation-related jobs for local folk in these crofting communities. In the short-term it is easier to fill any such jobs by the standard practice of wide-scale advertising, national interviews, and selection of the candidate with the most appropriate qualifications on paper. But this ignores the long-term social and psychological consequences of 'importing' a 'specialist' class with different values, different history, and perhaps a different language into close-knit but fragile rural communities. In the immediate future it would well repay the conservation movement to enter into a loose training partnership with a wide range of community leaders in order to educate both sides to the ways of crofting, the needs of conservation, and the legal complexities and potential benefits to both sides. In this way the land*users* (not simply land*owners*) would be able to act ever more effectively as custodians of the agricultural *and* conservation value of their land, instead of being constantly coaxed and cajoled into increasing their agricultural effectiveness alone.

The overriding reason why so-called 'market forces' encourage agricultural development at the expense of conservation, is that the agricultural side of crofting *provides rural communities with a recogniseable income,* however small, whereas the contribution of conservation to the rural economy is much harder to quantify in terms of hard cash. In most cases it is only indirect, such as through the development of tourism, student research parties, etc. and as such it is both sporadic and difficult to attribute to the efforts of any single organisation. This is where there needs to be a fundamental change in any sincere attempt to develop a truly integrated Development Policy.

Many landusers are still not aware that in cases where the NCC decide to impose restrictions on certain types of activities, they are obliged to pay a management grant to compensate the owner/occupier for the potential loss of income which would result from the abandonment of the proposed development. For example, an area of bogland may be a pain in the neck to a crofter who cannot use it for grazing, and may even, occasionally, lose a beast in it. This area may however be a very good site for wildlife, and if the NCC object to the crofter's plan to drain the area in order to create better grazing, and if a compromise solution cannot be worked out, the crofter may get a management grant to compensate for the increased income which he would have had if the grazing improvement scheme had gone ahead. This is fair enough in the short-term until we *all* get our act together to decide what we mean by 'integrated landuse', but really it is a far from ideal situation. The very idea of compensation implies that the land *should* be put to agricultural use, and that the grant is in some way a 'handout' for doing nothing with this piece of land. This is not an idea which will sit well with people who are traditionally used to *working the land*. In any event the management grant will be paid as a value of the loss of *agricultural* land which we would all agree is of 'marginal' quality, with *poor* soil, bad terrain, adverse weather, problems of accessibility, and distance from markets, with little realistic hope of significant improvement. At the same time it is being said that the land is exceedingly *valuable* in terms of its conservation potential − *so this is the value that should be paid*.

It is time that we came to terms with the idea of conservation as a cash crop − as a product of a certain type of *managed* landuse system, and that for those crofters and upland farmers who, by their very methods of working, operate in a manner which is beneficial to the natural environment should be rewarded. Let us have an end to snide remarks at 'primitive' agriculture, at 'uneconomic' systems, and at 'unworkable' practices − it is these very systems which have ensured for so long the quality of so much of the natural environment of the Highlands and Islands while it was being lost elsewhere. In fact it can further be argued that in communities where croft land has been neglected or allowed to fall into misuse (for whatever reason), the resulting deterioration in the crofting system is often closely paralleled by a deterioration in the wildlife potential. Active resumption of traditional crofting practices and their modern equivalents (*Nobody* would *choose* to plough with a cascrom these days!), will rejuvenate the land, the community and the dependent wildlife.

In this respect it is important to notice that I say that the 'conservation grants' should be paid to the land*user*, not simply the person (or syndicate) who happens to be in possession of the title deeds! It is a system which has been created by the land*user* (often with little or no help, and often in spite of downright obstruction from the landowner), and it is the land*user* who must have the incentive to continue operating in an environmentally beneficial manner, despite the other inducements towards agricultural intensification and specialisation. For crofters in particular we need to see the removal of the archaic laws which govern the ownership of trees on croftland by the estate owner *no matter who has planted them*. Trees and conservation should be like any other product of the land, turnips, potatoes, hay, etc., and should entitle the person who is producing that crop to realise the fruits of his/her labours.

The idea of conservation as a crop however presents further difficulties, for unlike turnips or potatoes the 'conservation crop' of a piece of land cannot be sold to consumers in a city market place. We need to find a way to make the city dwellers pay for the benefits provided by the crofter or upland farmer. We need to end this hit-and-miss system of land management which makes conservation depend on the benevolence of the landuser in the face of conflicting incentives. We need to provide annual 'conservation management grants' to all those engaged in environmentally beneficial landuse, not just those who are lucky enough to have little islands of SSSI within their land. This conservation cash crop could be provided by special tax incentives such as private forestry is well used to receiving; or by special payments for certain agreed practices which although environmentally beneficial may not be considered generally as 'economically feasible' as other common practices. These could be a bonus premium for a good cattle/sheep ratio on crofts, which would discourage crofters from getting rid of cattle and would maintain the grazing in better condition than would be the case under sheep alone. There could be special incentives for using local seaweed as fertiliser, and for the proper maintenance of previously 'improved' areas rather than simply the creation of more reseeded moorland. There could be schemes to encourage the aged crofter, who is no longer able to work his croft to the full, and to pass it over to a younger, more active person, designated by the crofter, who would be able to keep the land in good heart. Financial encouragement could be given to diversify crofting activities into small scale forestry (ideally on a community basis), and horticulture.

There is a very good case for urging the creation of new crofts on present estate land, bringing in new families and re-instilling a vitality in our rural communities. In such cases we are dealing with the conservation of rural communities as well as of wildlife, and if these communities are allowed to become even more depopulated than they are at present then the land will fall into disuse, and in many cases the wildlife will also suffer.

A move must be made towards farm diversification, not solely agricultural diversification, following the lead already given by crofting. Instead of farmers pushing the land harder and harder in order to stay up with the competition and the increasingly keen prices, farmers will need to obtain part of their family income from activities other than pure agriculture, while still living in, and working on the farm. In this, farm-forestry and farm-conservation are only two of several options.

What lies at the bottom of all this though is the clear realisation that there can be no real political democracy without economic democracy, and that despite two hundred years of change from a clan society, the root cause of the problem lies with our outmoded system of landownership in Scotland. I firmly believe that 'The Highland Problem' and many other so-called conflicts between crofting, conservation, forestry, agriculture, and urban development, are no more than red herrings on the cold slab of landownership. We should press first for a compulsory, publicly accessible register of landownership and landuse in Scotland which would be constantly updated, and would serve as a baseline for the development of a logical integrated landuse policy. We need to know what is in the shop before we can know what our surpluses, shortages, and resource priorities are. Without this, landuse planning and the physical development of rural communities in a lasting and meaningful way, are pie-in-the-sky. The devolution of power does not stop with the right to vote in a government of your choice, nor does merely exchanging a foreign landowner for a Scottish one solve any major problems — to pretend it does merely creates extra problems. We *must* have greater public participation and community ownership of land as a basic resource. The model of the Stornoway Trust with its system of elected Trustees could serve as a model for community democracy, but there are others.

The Place of Trees in the Highlands

By ROBIN CALLANDER

The Highlands and the Lowlands are the two halves of mainland Scotland, each covering over 8 million acres (3.3 m.ha.). The boundary between them follows the Highland Boundary Fault and the eastern edge of the Grampian Mountains. This is a natural frontier that coincides with a major change in the ecological character of naturally occurring or native woodlands.

The Highlands are the only part of Britain where there are the boreal woodlands typical of northern latitudes. This type of woodlands represents the natural tree cover throughout most of the Highlands, with Scots Pine and birch as the main tree species. Scots Pine does not occur naturally elsewhere in Britain and birch is only a naturally dominant component of native woodlands in the Highlands. Oakwoods, which are the main form of native woodland for the rest of Britain, only have a limited distribution in the Highlands.

The native woodlands that still exist in Britain are small and scattered fragments of their original extent. However, extensive native woodlands survived much later in the Highlands than in any other region of Britain. Then, in comparison to the centuries of attrition elsewhere, the native woodlands in the Highlands suffered a period of intense exploitation.[1] The consequences of this episode have been described by Fraser Darling as 'the biggest effect Man has exerted on the history of the Highlands'.[2]

The boreal character of the woodland environment and the different native woodland history, are important aspects of the distinctive place of trees in the Highlands. This paper starts with the historical background and then describes the expansion of conifer plantations in the Highlands, before examining some of the ways in which trees could make a greater contribution to the future of rural communities in the Highlands.

NATIVE WOODLAND HISTORY

The Highlands were colonised by the present native tree species after the last Ice Age. Subsequent climatic fluctuations altered the extent of native woodlands and local environmental factors have always excluded trees from many areas. However, estimates suggest that native woodlands covered over 50 per cent of the Highlands at the beginning of the present climatic period circa 500 BC. These woodlands had been established for over six thousand years by then and they remained remarkably unaltered for the next two thousand years until the beginning of the 17th century. Collectively labelled the Caledonian Forest or Great Wood of Caledon, 'The Highland Forests at this time were still more or less intact'.[3]

These extensive native woodlands had survived for two main reasons. Firstly, the Highlands did not have the wood intensive industries or burgh development of lowland regions and the pastoral agriculture of the subsistence economy had only a limited impact. Secondly, the isolation, not simply remoteness, of the Highlands meant there had been little external exploitation of the Caledonian Forest. For example, the Roman and English armies had only skirted the edge of the Highlands and no Royal Forests or Church lands were established. Bears and beavers were amongst the forest animals in the Highlands for much longer than in the South.[4] These species had been extinct for many centuries in England, where the native woodlands had long been reduced to isolated and intensively managed pockets.

The exploitation of the valuable forest resources in the Highlands resulted from timber and fuelwood shortages in England and Lowland Scotland. The exploitation started throughout the Highlands in the early decades of the 17th century and reached a peak in the 18th century after the suppression of the Jacobites. There was at that time 'the promise of material rewards for the exploiter of Highland resources on a scale quite without parallel in previous history'.[5] The exploitation was based almost exclusively on blast-furnace iron smelting in the west and on water-powered sawmilling for timber in the east. The first examples of each enterprise were set up by Englishmen and throughout the period of exploitation, the great majority of the products went to England. This externally based exploitation ended in the first half of the 19th century, by which time the remaining fragments of native woodland covered only about 2 per cent of the Highlands.

At the beginning of this episode in the early 17th century, the Highlands had been a near-autonomous region, a scarcely visited northern frontier zone, mountainous with forests, where the people spoke a 'foreign' language and had a warlike reputation. By the end, the Highlands had been reduced to a peripheral part of the British State with a pattern of social conditions and land uses that still dominate the Highlands today. The exploitation of the native woodlands was first in a series of sweeping landuse changes that date from that time. It was followed by a 'boom and bust' cycle in the traditional cattle trade, which built up rapidly during the late 18th century and declined steeply in the early 19th century. The sheep industry, which had been introduced from the 1760s, expanded swiftly and replaced the cattle trade before passing its peak by the 1870s. Deer forests, which first appeared in the second half of the 18th century, were by that time multiplying towards their maximum extent in the early decades of this century. Since then, afforestation with conifer plantations, which also first emerged in the 18th century, has been spreading at an increasing rate, with the fastest expansion in recent decades.

PLANTATION FORESTRY

Towards the end of the period of native woodland exploitation, landowners in the Highlands started to manage some woodlands on a regular basis. Birch, the traditional tree of the Highland economy, was not included within these new forestry practises and by the 1850s the coppice management of oakwoods had been abandoned. This left forestry in the Highlands almost exclusively concerned with conifer plantations. Some of these incorporated the remnants of native pinewoods, but most had been established by enclosing and planting bare ground. These plantations were progressively thinned as they grew and then clear felled. By the 1850s, these plantations were more extensive than the native woodlands in the Highlands. However, as about 60 per cent of the trees in these plantations consisted of the Highlands' native conifer (Scots Pine), native trees, self-sown and planted, were still predominant in the landscape.[6]

This pattern of plantations remained broadly the same until the creation of the Forestry Commission (1919) and the introduction of public subsidies for private forestry (1921). The area of conifer plantations and the use of introduced or exotic conifers then started to increase. Since the 1940s, there has been a very rapid acceleration in both these trends. Conifer plantations now cover 10 per cent of the Highlands, double their area at the beginning of the century. The use of exotic conifers has risen to over 90 per cent, with over 75 per cent of the trees planted each year in the Highlands now consisting of one species of North American conifer, Sitka Spruce. These plantations are usually felled on short rotations of about 40 years and 89 per cent of the trees in Highland

plantations are less than 45 years old. These uniform plantations, with their restricted species composition and age structure, have high establishment costs, but are managed to
produce a narrow band of cash crops for distant markets.

The rapid spread of these single purpose plantations has
been promoted by successive governments to expand Britain's
home grown supplies. Support has been aimed at 60,000
acres (25,000 ha.) of new plantations each year and these will
continue to be concentrated within Scotland. Eighty five per
cent of all trees planted in Britain during the last ten years
have been in Scotland and Scotland contains a similar
percentage of the land considered suitable for afforestation.
Scotland, with a third of Britain's land area, already accounts
for 50 per cent of all Britain's woodlands and wood production. These shares are increasing rapidly through afforestation,
and within Scotland the Highlands will be used to accom-
modate most of this expansion.

The proportion of native trees in the Highland landscape
has been halved in the last sixty years to less than a third of the
tree cover. This mainly results from the decline in the use of
Scots Pine in plantations. Self-sown native woodlands,
though now only about 10 per cent of the tree cover, still
cover approximately 2 per cent of the Highlands.[7] More than
90 per cent of these native woodlands have survived without
being managed, while exploitive felling, overgrazing and
underplanting with conifers, have caused serious declines in
their species composition, condition and distribution. The
overall area of native woodlands has only been maintained
against these pressures by birch and pine. These boreal species
have a pioneer capacity to colonise bare ground and, in the
districts with most birch and pine, young stands have tended
just to compensate for losses. However, many of these woods
are themselves prevented from regenerating and most are
located in areas where they are likely to be replaced by the
expansion of exotic conifer plantations.

The natural tendency of these two boreal species to shift their stances, is also at odds with the Nature Conservancy Council's 'Ancient Woodlands' policy. This policy to conserve Britain's native woodlands is the result of experience in England, where continuous site occupation is the main ecological feature of native woodlands. As a result, the distinctive boreal woodlands of the Highlands, which still include Britain's largest and most natural native woodlands, will be largely excluded from appropriate management.

The few native woodlands in nature reserves in the Highlands are usually managed without the use of planting or felling. Remarkably, this approach, which excludes any timber or wood production, is virtually the only system of woodland management found in the Highlands, other than the single purpose plantation forestry described above. The lack of forestry practises between these two extremes has resulted in confusion over the use of the term 'forestry'. 'Forestry' is the art and science of managing trees and embraces all forms of sustainable woodland management. However, the near complete dominance of the present plantation regime in the Highlands, has led to this specific type of forestry being described as if it were synonomous with 'forestry' itself.

The many critics of the present plantation regime have often been amongst those perpetuating this misuse of terms and so have inadvertently hindered the discussion of alternatives. Their criticisms have principally questioned its economic value, the forms and level of public subsidies, its adverse relationship to other landuses and the high degree of environmental damage. There is also an increasing awareness of the lack of involvement and benefit to rural communities, despite the continued use of 'support for rural communities' as an important justification for the expansion of this forestry regime with public subsidies.

All trees, whether planted or self-sown, belong in Scotland's

Land Laws to the owner of the ground upon which they are growing. Within the concentrated pattern of landownership in the Highlands, this means that rural communities, including agricultural tenants and crofters, have very little involvement with trees. These communities gain no direct financial benefit from either the public funds and fiscal concessions given to private forestry or the multi-million pound value of public and private forestry enterprises in the Highlands. Beyond this, rural communities also derive little employment or other local economic benefit from the present forestry regime. The centralisation, mechanisation and other labour saving strategies developed by this single purpose system, mean that employment in forestry has been falling despite the major expansion of plantations and harvesting volumes. The increases in production have maintained employment levels in wood processing industries, but these have moved to large-scale factories away from rural areas.

Afforestation with exotic conifers in the Highlands relies on both artificial subsidies and externally based, mobile investment capital. This suggests that this single purpose form of forestry will follow the pattern of other landuse surges in the Highlands during the last 250 years and decline.

TREES FOR THE HIGHLANDS

Much of the Highlands is a landscape that would naturally grow trees and there can be little doubt that trees could have a vital role in a viable future for many local communities. However, there are two main prerequisites for the successful contribution of trees to rural development in the Highlands.

The first is a high degree of local control and management. This requires a legislative redistribution of land rights, in which the ability of farmers and crofters to plant and manage trees on their land needs to be only one change in wider moves to diversify the involvement of rural communities with trees.

If this opportunity is opened up to rural communities, there will be the potential for the management of trees and woodlands to make the contributions, upon which rural development will depend, to local economies and employment.

The second requirement is a diversification of forestry practises in the Highlands. This would reinstate the genuine meaning of 'forestry' and need to be linked to a retargeting of government forestry policies. Local control and management will rely on using trees and woods for a wider range of products and purposes than at present. For example, production could be aimed towards a spectrum of uses, from meeting material needs on individual holdings and within the local community, to supplying local processing enterprises and wider markets of regional or national significance. The value of the individual woods and their local patterns would themselves be multipurpose through their contribution to other local landuses. For example, by providing materials, shelter and game and wildlife habitats, by sharing fences, tracks, equipment and other resources, and by contributing to local recreational opportunities and landscape quality.

The development of this multi-purpose approach to forestry would diversify and strengthen local incomes and the rural economy. Its viability would rely on its locality basis and flexibility, in contrast to the present single purpose regime's dependence on subsidies and standardisation. Viability, which is always difficult to interpret for the time-scale of trees and woodlands, has a different context in peripheral communities utilising their own resources, including land and labour. The seasonal requirements of forestry work complement the patterns of other landuses and part-time rural employment, and are also well suited to partnerships or cooperation between neighbours and the sharing of specialised equipment. Woodland management also uses some of the skills and equipment that already exist in agricultural communities. Investment is still required to create new woodlands, even if land is locally available. However, strategies are available to local communities that would remove many of the high capital costs associated with establishing the present conifer plantations, and the rest could be severely reduced.

The dispersal of forestry control to rural communities and the diversification of forestry practises by them, will inevitably result in an increased use of the tree species native to the Highlands. Firstly, the local provenances of these species offer a range of trees that are best suited to the bioclimatic conditions of each locality where trees might be expected to grow in the Highlands. Secondly, the ecology and potential products of these species are well adapted to the types of low input, continuous yield systems upon which the rural management of forestry will mainly depend. These systems will need to utilise a range of types of mixed species, mixed aged, permenant woodlands. However, this rural forestry will be based primarily on the management options and product range offered by birch and pine. Over most of the Highlands, no broadleaved tree can match the potential of birch and, on genuine conifer sites, Scots Pine is the most viable species for rural forestry. The many attributes of these two boreal species provide rural communities in the Highlands with forestry opportunities that can not be equalled elsewhere in Britain.

An increase in native trees from their present low ebb towards a new predominance in the Highlands and a re-establishment of birch's contribution to the region's rural economy, would be important measures of the progress of locality based, rural forestry. However, any use or development of native trees needs to give appropriate recognition to the existing, genuinely native woodlands. The integrity of their genetic composition and reproduction by natural means for over eight thousand years, is a valuable asset to conserve in its own right. These surviving wild trees and woods in the Highlands do have an important productive potential, but the utilisation of this needs to respect the essential character of the resource.

The Highland landscape has characteristic patterns for the use of trees and woods. These would guide the distribution of types and sizes of woods, including their integration with other landuses and the form of their individual management. These arrangements would also provide the basis in each locality for the levels of control and involvement within the community. Individuals could have different kinds of participation in several types of management systems at a range of sites. This need be no more exceptional than someone who works a croft, contributing to a local farm and having a share in common hill land.

The future of many Highland communities is likely to remain closely related to the use of their local natural resources. At present, the use of the Highlands for forestry does not coincide with the use of forestry for the Highlands. However, trees could have a vital place in sustained rural development, if they are the right trees in the right places, managed by the right methods and the right means.

NOTES

1. Exploitation: the intermittant or sustained removal of timber or other woodland products without regard to the replacement of losses.

2. Fraser Darling, *West Highland Survey*, Oxford, 1955.

3. Professor Carlisle in *The Native Pinewoods of Scotland*, I.T.E., 1975.

4. There is a lack of modern work on the historical status of these and other species.

5. Professor Smout, *A History of the Scottish People*, Collins, 1969.

6. Historical woodland statistics are inaccurate compared to the results of modern surveys and neither tend to be based on the Highlands as defined here. Historical figures are only given here as indications and all Highlands statistics usually as estimates.

7. There are no overall surveys of native woodlands for Scotland or the Highlands.

Access

By RENNIE McOWAN

It is frequently said that there is no law of trespass in Scotland, but that statement is technically and legally inaccurate. The reason that it is so widely uttered and believed is because a *moral* freedom-to-roam in wild places in Scotland is a fact, provided it is accompanied by countryside manners and sensibilities. Although the *de jure* position is grey, the *de facto* position tends to operate almost as if it were enshrined by law. I believe that this situation is now threatened.

The mere fact of being on wild land is not, by itself, an offence in Scotland. But all land belongs to someone, and Scots law states that the owner has the right to ask a walker to leave his land, and may use just sufficient force to achieve that object. Such instances are extremely rare, and in thirty years of hill tramping and climbing in Scotland, I have never come across a situation in which request and force were successfully combined.

To prevent a walker entering his land, a landowner has to seek an interdict in a civil court, and this would not be granted unless potential damage could be proved. Since no damage is caused by walking over wild land, except perhaps during the peak of the stalking season, such actions which would be expensive and time consuming, rarely occur. In fact, however, most landowners understand the desire of walkers to roam, and most outdoor people recognise the need for caution and occasionally consultation during the lambing, grouse-shooting and deer stalking seasons. There are some exceptions to this, but, in modern times a kind of co-existence has grown up, amiable and open, with both parties reasonably satisfied most of the time. It is this mutual tolerance which is under threat.

There are two other legal points which need to be clarified, and then set aside as they are not part of the main debate. It is a criminal offence in Scotland to light a fire, and to camp without the landowner's permission. However, the latter point is covered by 19th century legislation which was mainly intended to be used against the tinkers, or travelling people. Hill wanderers, setting down a tent in some lonely spot for one night and then moving on are not likely to be affected, but in theory could be.

Attempts to restrict the walker's freedom-to-roam began in a formal way with the birth of the big sporting estates in the 19th century, and have continued since. At that time, although very real prohibitions were in force, organisations like the Scottish Mountaineering Club tended not to test the general issue. However some noteworthy battles were fought over rights-of-way (established routes of antiquity, protected by law and normally connecting specific places). In 1847 a clash in Glen Tilt between the Duke of Athole's gillies and a party of botanists led to much publicity and litigation. This succeeded in clarifying the law in general and the Tilt right of way in particular. However, the Duke of Athole was well known as an irascible autocrat, and the Tilt incident has to be seen against that background. In 1867 John Stuart Blackie, professor of Greek at Edinburgh University, climbed the Buachaille Etive Mor contrary to the wishes of the proprietor. Afterwards he called on the Fiscal at Fort William, shared some port with him, and was informed that he was to be prosecuted. Later sterling action by the Scottish Rights of Way Society led to the expensive but successful action over the Jock's Road route in Glen Doll. At the Parliamentary level, James Bryce, MP (later Viscount Bryce) president of the Cairngorm Club, campaigned for free access to mountains.

These moves, from prohibitions by landowners to a legal clarification of rights-of-way, led to a vigorous demand for the right to roam. The great hiking and outdoor boom of the thirties when many unemployed men and women made their way on foot, by bicycle, or by hitch-hiking, from the cities to the hills, walking and climbing at will, and sleeping under hedges, in caves, or in home-made howffs in lonely glens, underlined the *de facto* situation of a public belief in the right of freedom-to-roam. There were, sadly, clashes with some landowners, mainly because of fires and illegal use of empty cottages and bothies, but the desire to walk and climb could not be stopped by the law and carried on unabated. More recently, the attitude of those returning from the Second World War, having spent their best years fighting tyrants, and being in no mood to accept dictatorship at home, ensured that the moral freedom-to-roam has become an indelible part of Scottish public opinion, and will not now be challenged without uproar.

In spite of all this, I believe that the threats to our freedom-to-roam are real and will intensify.

Land forbidden to all for defence purposes is a fact of life in all European countries, but in Scotland it has already reached an extent previously unknown in peacetime, and may be greatly increased if the ELF proposals go ahead.

Changes in countryside legislation and local authority responsibilities have led to 'access agreements', the signposting of paths, and the introduction of 'Ways' into Scotland. These are well meant, but carry problems with them. The 'Ways', official long distance footpaths, were born out of English countryside pressures, but in Scotland they are controversial because they can create a climate of opinion which conveys the impression that it is improper to deviate from the route. 'Ways' are promoted by The Countryside Commission for Scotland – the Government's agent. The Local Authorities then erect signposts, but may take it upon themselves to attach further notices asking people to stick to the paths. If a network of 'Ways' is established in Scotland, we might ultimately come to a situation where to stray from the 'official' route is frowned upon, or even banned by law. Access agreements between a landowner and a local authority can serve a useful purpose when they deal with specific visitor pressure at some sensitive point, and that is valid. Too often however it leads to a ban on walking on any neighbouring ground.

The growth of forestry, especially private forestry, with its necessary and expensive fencing, brings with it severe restrictions on freedom-to-roam. The Forestry Commission at least makes some provision for recreation, but private forestry has no such legal responsibility. It is in this field that the need for some kind of statutory period for public consultation and planning controls, before tracts of hill land are planted in trees, is most acute.

The growth of country parks, normally fairly urban in character, has a useful role, although their countryside character is sometimes ridiculously over-portrayed. There is a danger, however, that their establishment may lead to calls for more such parks, copied from the English examples, in the wild areas of Scotland. It might be that Scotland could benefit from such parks, but not if they mean importing English attitudes to the law of trespass and freedom-to-roam, nor if, because of English population pressure, Scottish parks are considered only as fossilised playgrounds for the visitors from the overcrowded South. The whole question of development and conservation is considered in another article in this Paper. Suffice it to say that it is possible in Scotland to have lonely and beautiful wilderness existing alongside glens, straths and coasts which sustain living thriving communities.

Many Scots are complacent about their rights on the hills. Despite its good work and venerable character the Scottish Rights of Way Society has only a small membership. This is probably because most of the outdoor population feel that it is not sufficiently relevant. Since their right of way is everywhere provided no damage is caused and no privacy invaded, they see no need to protect 'legal' rights of way. On the other hand much of the pressure for conservation and the establishment of national parks comes from English people who do not appreciate the legal differences in Scotland, and who have contributed a creeping anglicisation to our outdoor traditions. In a draft document from a prominent outdoor organisation, it was stated that the moral right in Scotland to deviate from rights-of-way existed in Scotland *solely* because of the tolerance of landowners. Another example was the access booklet produced recently by the Mountaineering Council of Scotland and the Scottish Landowners Federation which supported the efforts of certain estates to confine walkers to defined routes, and prohibit access to large areas of ground during the hind-shooting season (October 21st to February 15th) a period in which cull shooting is very spasmodic as well as the stag season (July 1st to October 2nd). In both these cases appropriate amendments were made, but the drift is clear.

We have no need of English influences in Scotland. We have one of the best people/land/resources profiles in Europe; a large land mass, much of it wild, and a relatively small population. Other such countries have their citizens' freedom-to-roam enshrined in law (accompanied by stringent penalties for damage, litter and the invasion of privacy). We need to be vigilant that any attempt to change the law will be for the better. Without a Parliament in Scotland this will be difficult to achieve.

Crofting – Is There a Future?

By ANGUS McHATTIE

THE PAST

The crofting counties have had a complex history which it is not the purpose of this paper to unravel, save to explain that the 1886 Act gave crofters the security of tenure previously denied them. This effectively put a stop to the landlords exerting excessive pressure on the horrifically poor inhabitants to pay extortionate rents.

The Act was responsible for halting the clearances which in the preceeding 100 years had reduced the population of Skye from over 40,000 to about 20,000. Since 1886 the population has dropped even further to about 8,400 (1981 Census), but appears now to be stabilising.

The population structure has also changed with time, and is now in a perilous position with an increasing proportion (more than 25 per cent) over retiral age. This is potentially disasterous for an area with a way of life that is demanding both physically and mentally.

But in celebrating the centenary of the 1886 Act, let us not dwell over long upon the past, with its memories and scant-healed scars. For too long the Highlander has lived in the past with all the maudlin notions that go with this. Let us certainly learn from the past, and use the knowledge to plan for future improvement and development.

THE PRESENT

Crofting until recently appeared to be in limbo. The lack of any detailed plans for the future at both local and national

44

level has ensured that the system only reacts to events after they occur. No one has put thought to the mechanisms required for the future. For example tourism has for years been seen as the saviour of the crofting areas, but not enough has been done to encourage it, and so we do not supply adequate wet-weather facilities, quality entertainment, provisioning etc. Compare this to an example of Scandinavian forward planning. The Monkstadt Oil Refinery, north of Bergen, was to undergo an extension in the Spring of 1986. Nearly two years before the event, in the summer of 1984, the local agricultural committee was deciding on who would benefit from the pigswill from the canteen, the surplus oil, rockfill etc.

Perhaps crofting needed the jolt of its approaching centenary for it to get the notion that without action the limbo would not be just a passing phase. The birth of the Scottish Crofters' Union (SCU) has shown that a great many people (3000 members by 1985) are committed to action and to establishing an organisation that can plan and form coherent policies for the next 100 years.

THE FUTURE

In the wider view of the EEC crofting is a viable way by which to hold people in remote rural areas. To consider the area without the web of crofting activity that holds the communities together is to think of a true wilderness area, devoid of people except for a few isolated communities based on tourism, fishing etc., comparable to, and perhaps as poignant as, the tundra to which it sometimes feels similar. The effect of crofting on the structure of the Highland economy is disproportionate to the approximate ten per cent employment that it generates. The way of life means almost all to the area. Even those who have never had stock or worked a croft in the true sense feel a strong bond to crofting, and that counts for a great deal.

There are two policy areas that require urgent attention. The first is forestry – can we get an integrated forest policy for the Highlands, with crofters' hands at the helm? We need the shelter, warmth, and the economic benefits that go with forestry, but which, due to the tenancy system are at present denied to us. We must let forest plantations be treated as a farm crop and as such be the property of the tenant, not as at present, the landlord. In Norway I spoke at length about this aspect of the crofting tenant-landlord system, and asked of a similar system there. The answer was that it had died out in the 13th century!

Secondly we need to examine the landownership problem more fully than has been done so far. We cannot have the situation, which existed in Waternish in Skye in the late 1970s and early 1980s, when, due to the activities of Dutch land speculators the crofters did not know, and some may still not know, who their landlord was. Some of them were also put in a position of a 'Take it or leave it, once or never', deal to buy their croft land. This has resulted in some of them losing out on their grant assistance as outlined below. Whatever comes of the present uncertainty in agriculture in the EEC, we must press for the change necessary to extract the land from the clutches of the privileged few, who have maintained their hold down through the centuries.

We need to examine the 1976 Crofting Act which was meant to encourage investment by enabling crofters to buy their land, and so become eligible for mortgages etc. which were previously denied them. There was also scope for some land conveyancing. This is an area which I feel has been over-exploited. Good, hard won arable land is lost to housing and amenity land, and viable units are decreased in size and become uneconomic. There is also the question of where this available capital has gone. There is not much sign of its investment in land improvement.

A problem for those who have purchased their land is that

they have found themselves as landowners, and so means-tested, and for those with other sources of income, debarred from the Crofter Counties Agricultural Grants Scheme. Without the access to the higher rate of grant, the marginal nature of the land and enterprise does not encourage investment. This leads to the cycle of neglect as the land become unworked and unproductive.

We have now witnessed some trading amongst crofters and others of the crofts themselves. This has led to an unprecedented rise in the market price of a croft – to a level far above its true value. This mitigates against the aspiring young crofter, and effectively puts these crofts into the hands of the 'white settler', or as bad, if not worse the retiring expatriot. This is the type of activity we abhor in landlords, so why is there no hue and cry when a croft is sold or assigned to another party who is unsuited due to age, experience etc? In the free market, it seems, finance rules all.

What then are relevant examples of workable systems of land tenancy or stewardship? (I feel that we do not own this land, but are tolerated by it, and sometimes only just!) The various attempts at involving public bodies, e.g. the Department of Agriculture and Fisheries for Scotland (DAFS) and the Highlands and Islands Development Board (HIDB) in landownership, though they promised much, have not been very successful. DAFS is, on Skye, a major landowner, but evidence of unworked crofts, of absenteeism and neglect, abound just as much on the DAFS estates as on those in private ownership. The HIDB do have powers to obtain land, but seem paralysed. When the estates of Knoydart and Killilan, which were eminently suitable to be split into viable crofts and hill farms, came on the market, the HIDB allowed the opportunity to pass, in spite of strong local pressure to buy. Government bodies in the Highlands seem to have a marked unwillingness to grasp the thorny problems of land-ownership. All of them, DAFS, HIDB, and the Crofters'

Commission, seem hell-bent on the path of least resistance, and when forced to make a decision, always, it appears, come down against the crofter. Killilan estate is now owned by an Arab enterprise which concentrates on sport. Knoydart has now been subdivided, not among crofters, but among various millionaires based south of the Tees-Exe line. At least Knoydart did not fall to the military, whose presence is now quite unprecedented since the Second World War. This expansion must be halted before it gets totally out of hand.

The Stornoway Trust is one example of how croft land can be managed from within, and it is examined elsewhere. However, the example of the owner occupied Glendale estate does not have much to commend it.

There has to be some arrangement to ensure that owners live on and work the land. Here again we may look to Norway, where it is a requirement that those who purchase (or otherwise obtain) land must live for two years within five miles of the land. This has ensured that the land is used. There is a healthy rural climate, despite countless second or third homes, and no public sector housing to speak of. There are no waiting lists, poor quality housing or ghettoes. Rural housing is scattered and individualistic, not restricted to straight lines and clumps as in the North West Highlands. Adequate forest cover helps break up the landscape and to hide or enhance buildings or development.

On returning from Norway to Skye recently, I had occasion to compare the view from similar 3000ft granite hills in both countries. In Norway the valley I looked down upon contained an autonomous village of 20 small farms, with their own crops, power supply, school etc. — a prosperous and happy place with a good trade surplus and a population with a healthy age structure. The Skye valley had twenty blackface ewes and twelve lambs. Compared to what the Norwegians started with, we are sitting on a gold mine. The development potential in the Highlands and Islands is immense.

After two years of being involved in trying to put this message across to a wide range of people at all levels, I still think that there is a gold mine. What I am not sure about is whether there is the will to go out and take the initiative, to develop, to gain self confidence, and put the past 100 years where it belongs — firmly behind us. Let us take the first step towards a viable, healthy industrious rural population in the crofting areas, towards a population concerned not with exporting its talent and intellectual cream, but as circumstances are dictating already, to keeping them at home to develop the whole area as an entity. Let us at last lay claim to the stewardship of the land without any of the drawbacks or snags of the past century.

Land in Community Ownership

Sixty years of the Stornoway Trust

By FRANK THOMPSON

ORIGIN

In May 1918 the ownership of the island of Lewis passed into the hands of Lord Leverhulme, one of the most enterprising, innovative and entrepreunerial industrialists in Britain. At the same time many returning ex-Servicemen from the 'war to end all wars' entertained fond hopes of achieving an ideal: the possession of some adequate plot of land to call their own, on which they could base a secure future for themselves and their families. In the event, they found themselves enmeshed in the repetition of an historical pattern which had occurred in the Highlands in previous centuries, when soldiers back from the Peninsular Wars and the Crimea found their homes razed to the ground, their families scattered and the land in the possession of proprietors who had other ideas for the use of their property.

To satisfy the need for plots of land, large farms were raided by crofters and cottars, the prime example being the island of Vatersay which eventually was divided up to create a new crofting community. The echoes of that and similar events buzzed in the heads of these Kaiser War veterans and were to become real situations which the new owner of Lewis, the 'bodach an t-shiabainn' (the soap man), had to face while he created his plans for making the island into a kind of industrial El Dorado based on fish processing.

The period between 1918 and 1923, when Leverhulme

pulled out of Lewis, is well documented and can be read in
Lord of the Isles by Nigel Nicolson (1960) and in the *Trans-
actions of the Gaelic Society of Inverness*. Suffice to say here that
Leverhulme decided in 1923 to abandon his schemes for
Lewis, leaving him with the question of how to dispose of the
island. Despite the bitter disappointment he obviously felt at
not being able to do 'something in a small way for the
permanent benefit of its fine people,' he decided to give Lewis
to its people.

Any crofter who wanted to become the owner of his acres
was open to accept his croft as a gift from Leverhulme. The
town of Stornoway, the Castle and its wooded policies, a large
acreage of moorland, and the crofting communities, was
to be given to the people of Stornoway. In the event the
crofters refused the offer. One crofter put the problem very
simply: 'The rent of my croft is £1 per annum. I pay 3/9d a
year in rates. If I become my own proprietor, what is to
hinder the Assessor putting a value of say £20 on my house?'
He would also have lost his security of a fixed rateable value
and lost access to grants and other funds available to crofting
activities.

On the other hand, the Town Council of Stornoway
accepted Leverhulme's gift, which consisted of Lews Castle
and its policies, the Parish of Stornoway (which extended
northwards from Arnish Moor as far as Tolsta, 14 miles
away), all the large farms and all the sporting and fishing
rights. The whole gift was to be administered by the Stornoway Trust.

COMMUNITY ESTATE OWNERSHIP

The Stornoway Trust is certainly unique in the Highlands
and probably in Britain. It is a body looking after an estate of
some 64,000 acres which is wholly in community ownership.
The Trustees are drawn from the community and are elected

by secret ballot by persons who appear in the current Valuation Roll as owning or occupying property on the Estate. This means that while the owner, or tenant, of a property has a vote, the rest of his family do not. Tenants of Comhairle nan Eilean (Western Isles Islands Council) within Stornoway parish have a vote just as surely as do the crofters on the Estate. The Trust is run by a Factor, a local man, who is the employee of the Trustees.

Until recently the Trust did little other than act as a caretaking body, despite the fact that it had powers to develop its assets. This was because the income was limited to that derived from interest on Security Investments, Royalties, and estate rents (in general croft rents have not been increased since 1886), and was sufficient only to cover the expenses of administration, and to maintain the Castle policies in reasonable condition. Thus funds for investment in major developments were not available.

Despite this lack of cash during its formative years, the Trust helped small developments by making land available at reasonable cost for housing and commercial purposes: individual house and garden sites, land for Local Authority housing, and land for such developments as builders yards, garages, hotels and the like.

Although the Trust is the landlord of a crofting estate, because of the very nature of the Trust, there has seldom been the difficult and strained relationships between crofter and landlord which has occurred, and still does, in areas where the land is under private ownership. Nevertheless, occasionally difficulties do occur, where, for instance, a crofter seeks to acquire land, which the Trust considers could be put to better community use.

The Trust has always held its door open to anyone who wanted advice, from either town or country, whether it was crofting advice, information on feus, legal advice and the like. This service has ever been free and available to all. It is a service which few crofters have on privately owned estates. The Trust saw the potential of Section 18 of the 1955 Crofting Act and promoted it at every opportunity, so that crofters were enabled to keep their houses and pass the croft on to, say, a son. It was because of the way the Trust was operating under that particular Section that it was retained in the 1976 Crofting Reform Act.

In recent years the financial situation of the Trust has improved as a result of the rents available from the on-shore, oil-related industrial activity at Arnish Point, at the mouth of Stornoway Harbour. This fresh influx of cash has enabled the Trust to launch a programme of activity which is now yielding impressive results, and will benefit the whole community.

The Trust has invested in a salmon hatchery and is involved in salmon sea-farming. These two developments promise to yield significant income for investment in other commercial areas. The Trust has given grant aid to Job Creation Projects sponsored by crofting townships. Financial encouragement has also been given to such projects as school educational trips, Gaelic choirs attending the National Mod, football teams, youth organisations and community halls. In this way the income generated by the Trust has been spread around to benefit the greatest number of people in the Trust's area. These things do not benefit the Trust financially, but are seen as worthy activities which offer general community benefits.

The need to develop land, particularly those areas which are at present under utilised, has always been on the Trustees' agenda, and it is one of the Trust's ambitions to initiate a pilot demonstration scheme of land improvement. Unfortunately current income does not allow for much activity on this front. However, should a crofting township come forward with a really imaginative and radical scheme for land improvement or development, the Trust would contribute financially. At present a small project is under way at Arnish with shelter belt afforestation, and the Trust is considering a small project based on the commercial exploitation of peat.

All in all, the Stornoway Trust has, over a period of six decades, developed a unique experience in land management, prosecuting a sympathetic attitude to the community ownership of land and towards its tenants.

The last word remains with the Trust Factor, Mr D. M. Smith to whom I am obliged for much of the information in this article: 'I do not see why funds from central Government should not be made availalble for the community ownership of land. I am confident that, provided those responsible got the geographical areas right, community ownership, not just for Lewis, could be the answer to many of the current problems which exist outside the Trust's area of responsibility, which means in effect the whole of the Highlands and Islands.'

The DAFS Crofting Estates:
A Case for Community Control?

By JAMES HUNTER

Those of us who have grown up in the West Highlands and Islands in the last 40 years or so have had a vague awareness that a good deal of land in our part of the country is owned by a more or less remote, but generally benevolent, landlord by the name of The Department – or, on more formal occasions, the Department of Agriculture and Fisheries for Scotland (DAFS).

Our schooling having usually neglected to include any worthwhile information about our locality's recent history, most of us have only a very sketchy idea of what brought about this state of affairs. Like the Free Church, DAFS is simply assumed to have always been a feature of life in crofting areas; the one being thought to be as immutable as the other.

Neither institution, as it happens, is all that old. But it is becoming increasingly apparent, thanks to ever more persuasive rumours about the next phase of the privatisation programme, that its ecclesiastical counterparts are better bets than DAFS in the longevity stakes – certainly as far as the Department's role as Highland landowner is concerned.

Now DAFS, strictly speaking, owns not a single acre. From its Chesser House bastion in Edinburgh's Gorgie Road, the Department simply administers a lot of land on behalf of that land's real proprietor, Her Majesty's Government in the person of Mr Malcolm Rifkind, Secretary of State for Scotland.

How Mr Rifkind came to hold sway over several hundred

thousand state-owned acres is a long story. It is also an instructive one; all the more instructive now that a proportion of these acres are hotly tipped candidates for disposal to private interests by means of procedures not dissimilar to those already adopted in the case of Forestry Commission land in Glen Affric and Glenelg.

The fact that so many crofters have the government as their landlord is not, to begin with, the result of some long-forgotten experiment in Socialism. Labour administrations have never been very keen on Highland land reform which, with the exception of some Liberal dabblings, has largely been the prerogative of governments controlled or dominated by Conservatives.

Thus it was in 1897 – some years before the Labour Party was formed and during the premiership of the impeccably Tory, Lord Salisbury – that the Cabinet set out on the reforming road that was to culminate in the state acquiring some 800,000 acres for settlement by crofters.

Ever since the frequently violent crofting protests of the 1880s it had been apparent that something would have to be done to satisfy the demand for land in the Highlands – a demand fuelled by the fact that the overcrowded crofting townships were invariably to be found next door to the enormous sheep farms created during the Clearances. A Liberal government had given crofters security of tenure in 1886. Eleven years later the Conservatives went one better. Now the land itself was to be redistributed by an agency established for the purpose: the Congested Districts Board.

Equipped with purchase powers far more extensive than the 1964 Labour government thought fit to grant the modern HIDB, the Congested Districts Board started work – appropriately enough – in Strathnaver, scene of the most notorious of all the Highland Clearances. There, in 1899, the Board bought the 12,000 acre Syre Estate from the Duke of Sutherland.

The following year the Board acquired 3000 acres in the vicinity of Eoligarry, Barra. In 1904 two more purchases were made — this time in Skye where the 20,000 acre Glendale Estate and the 45,000 acre Kilmuir Estate passed into public ownership. At this stage the intention was to hand that land on to owner-occupying crofters. No rents were paid by the smallholders who replaced sheep farmers on estates in the Board's possession. Instead the newly-settled crofters were to buy their crofts by making fifty annual payments to the government.

Only in Glendale did that arrangement continue — which is why Glendale is now owned by its crofters. Elsewhere, in 1911, the '50-year purchase' crofters on Congested Districts Board properties opted for tenancy — as opposed to owner-ship — in order to benefit from a variety of newly-introduced grants that were available only to agricultural tenants. That is why crofters in Eoligarry, Staffin and Syre — unlike those in Glendale — still pay rent to DAFS.

Also in 1911 the Congested Districts Board was itself wound up. In its place there was created the Board (sub-sequently rechristened the Department) of Agriculture for Scotland. The new Board inherited its predecessor's land-holdings in Sutherland and the Hebrides. It was also granted powers to speed up the land redistribution process — powers incorporated in a Land Settlement Act passed by the Liberal government of the day.

That Act enabled the Board of Agriculture to finance the creation of new crofts on land still in private ownership. This was done on an increasing scale. But it was clear by 1918 that, in the new circumstances resulting from the demand for land among men returning from military service in the First World War, a still more radical initiative was needed.

The result was the only real measure of land reform ever seen in Scotland, the Land Settlement Act of 1919 devised and implemented by the Lloyd-George coalition government

in which Conservatives were in an overwhelming majority.
The Act granted the Board of Agriculture a whole range of
compulsory purchase powers and the then enormous sum of
£3.5 million for settlement purposes.

Estate after estate and farm after farm were bought by the
Board. By the mid-1920s there were no sheep farms left in
the Western Isles. And in Skye some 60,000 acres had been
transferred to crofters. When the efforts of the Board of
Agriculture were added to those of the Congested Districts
Board, the net result — in the Highlands and Islands as a
whole — was the creation of 2776 new crofts and the en-
largement of another 5168.

It was a remarkable achievement. Its flavour is caught by
the experience of Syre in Strathnaver. When bought by the
Congested Districts Board in 1899 it provided employment
for two shepherds. Thirty years later 21 crofts had replaced
the original sheep farm. The cultivated area had risen from 6
acres to 232 acres. Cattle numbers were up from 4 to 158, and
sheep numbers from 1700 to 2163. And the human population had risen from 10 to 95.

Much the same was true of the other land settlement
estates. And the benefits continue to be felt today. Look at the
Staffin area of Skye, bought by the Congested Districts Board
eighty years ago. Compare it with a geographically similar area,
in Mull perhaps, where there was no land settlement. Certainly the Staffin crofts are smaller, more 'uneconomic' and
less 'viable' than a Mull sheep farm. But which locality
supports the more flourishing population?

'A crofting community,' concluded an official report com-
missioned by a Conservative government in the 1920s, 'is a
way of living and cannot be judged in terms of a profit and
loss account. The people were there and insisted on staying
there. Their conditions were a reproach to the nation of which
they form part, and the only way to remove that reproach was
to give them the available land.'

Although the Land Settlement Acts are still on the statute book – and could, in principle, be reactivated at any time – they have not been used since 1952 when Winston Churchill's government bought the Craignure Estate in Mull to resettle families evacuated from Soay. Now Mr Churchill's successors are inclined to dispose of all such assets; and the suspicion grows that the DAFS crofting estates, as the land settlement properties became known, will not for ever remain immune from Treasury pressure to sell whatever can be sold.

No institution is beyond reproach. And it may be that there is a good case for dismantling the Chesser House empire in the Highlands. Considering that the Kilmuir Estate, for example, was bought for under £2 an acre and that the average cost of a land settlement croft to the Treasury was £263, the return on the original investment ought certainly to be considerable – even allowing for DAFS administrative costs which were severely criticised by the House of Commons Public Accounts Committee some years ago.

Nor will DAFS crofting tenants be at risk as a result of an ownership change. They will have the same security as other crofters and the same right to buy their own holdings if they so wish.

But is the return to the land settlement estates to the traditional type of ownership really in accord with the objectives which led Mr Malcolm Rifkind's predecessors to acquire them in the first place? Is it even in accord with the government's own view of rural development as stated as recently as 1983.

'At the end of the day', said Mr Younger, the then Secretary of State for Scotland, 'the overriding objective must be to harness the creative energy and skills of people in local communities so that they will be able to maintain and enhance the life of these communities. What matters most is the encouragement of confidence in individuals and communities in their ability to tackle and overcome their problems in a practical way and to exploit their resources, both human and material.'

These are admirable sentiments. And any sale of the DAFS crofting estates will offer the ideal opportunity to put them into practice. Consider, for instance, the island of Vatersay, bought by the Congested Districts Board in 1909 for £6260. If it is to be sold, should the first offer not be made to the local community co-operative? What better way could there be of 'harnessing the creative energy and skills' of such a locality than making its people entirely responsible for its management? And is there not an analogy between such a concept and the procedures which have resulted in workforces being encouraged to take a substantial stake in those commercial enterprises which have already been privatised?

Just how community ownership might be effected is a matter for detailed discussion – although the Stornoway Trust, which manages an entire Hebridean parish on behalf of its inhabitants, provides one eminently satisfactory model. A Conservative government which is committed to promoting self-help and encouraging self-reliance would surely do well to approach any privatisation of the land settlement estates on the basis that they be privatised in the direction of their occupants.

The Authors

Dr ADAM WATSON, FRSE, is one of Scotland's foremost ecologists. He was brought up in Turriff, Aberdeenshire, and has liked exploring, mountaineering, skiing, and natural history since a boy. After study at Aberdeen University, he went to McGill University, Montreal, and was zoologist on the Arctic Institute's Baffin Island expedition. His main research has been on animal population regulation and social behaviour, but he has also studied the human impact on mountains, natural tree regeneration, and soil erosion on farmland. Formerly Officer in Charge of the Nature Conservancy's Mountain & Moorland Research Station, he is now Senior Principal Scientific Officer (Individual Merit) at the Institute of Terrestrial Ecology, Banchory. He has taken an interest in land-holding and land-use abroad, especially in North America, Scandinavia, Iceland, Switzerland and the Netherlands.

R. DRENNAN WATSON is a biologist who has worked in agriculture for many years advising farmers and teaching agricultural students about problems of crop protection. He has a wide interest in the conservation of wildlife and landscape, and is the current chairman of the North East Mountain Trust. He has developed a broad interest in landuse, especially in mountains and uplands, and has visited the mountainous regions of many countries. In 1982 he and Dr Adam Watson made a study tour of Switzerland, specifically to study the Swiss systems of landuse, and in 1985 he spent a short period in Sweden studying the same topic. Earlier this year he was awarded a Churchill Fellowship to travel in Western Europe and study systems of agro-forestry that might be applied to the Scottish uplands.

RENNIE McOWAN is a full time writer and lecturer, and has been hill walking in Scotland for over 30 years. He was a founder-member and first president of *The Scotsman* newspaper mountaineering club (now the Ptarmigan Club of Edinburgh), and is a founder member and archivist of the Scottish Wild Land Group.

He belongs to a number of outdoor and conservation bodies, including the Mountain Bothies Association, the National Trust for Scotland, the Scottish Rights of Way Society, and the Scottish Wildlife Trust.

His writings have appeared in the *Evening News, The Scots Magazine, The Scotsman,* and *The Glasgow Herald,* as well as many outdoor magazines. He has written a number of books, including, *Walks in the Trossachs and Rob Roy Country, Tales of Ben and Glen* and *The Man Who Bought Mountains,* and contributed to *Walking in Scotland.*

ROBIN FRASER CALLANDER lives in Aberdeenshire where he has a 3½ acre croft and is a member of a woodland management partnership that owns 1250 acres in Deeside. He is a professional drystane dyker, and regional publisher, and is the author of *Drystane Dyking in Deeside,* and the *History in the Birse* series. This series (4 volumes so far) examines the Deeside parish where Robin has his croft. Robin has made a particular study of landownership in Scotland, and his book on part of the research, *A Pattern of Landownership in Scotland,* will be published later this year. His other work includes heather thatching contracts, lecturing, and writing on a wide range of topics relating to rural Scotland. Since 1985 he has been Rural Forum's Project Consultant.

FRANK THOMPSON was brought up in Stornoway. After working elsewhere in England and Scotland, he is now back teaching in Lews Castle College. His interests are Highland-centred within the context of Scotland as a nation with an identifiable and viable culture. As a result he has been involved in Scottish national politics and the struggle to achieve statutory recognition for Gaelic. His interest in crofting has been lifelong. He has watched the changes in crofting and crofters brought about by the new regulations, and is convinced that the crofting way of life still provides a very valuable resource for Scotland, and perhaps the whole world. He is the author of many books, and has contributed to others, including the first Fletcher Paper: *Gaelic: Looking to the Future*.

ANGUS McHATTIE, aged 29, was brought up and educated in Skye. His crofting roots run deep, for his grandfather's family were cleared from an island in Loch Bracadale to make way for sheep. He now lives in Waterloo, Breakish, Skye, a township reckoned even by the Crofters' Commission to be one of the poorest settled areas in the North West Highlands. He is married to an Edinburgh girl who has totally embraced the crofting way of life, and provides the support necessary to enable the full time working of the croft. He has received two national awards to study crofting type agriculture in Scandinavia and its relevance to crofting in Scotland. He is Treasurer of the Scottish Crofters' Union, and its Skye Area President. His over-riding interest is the development of rural communities within the crofting areas.

Dr JAMES HUNTER was brought up in Duror, North Argyll, and educated at Oban High School, and at Aberdeen and Edinburgh universities. He is author of the widely acclaimed, 'The Making of the Crofting Community', which was based on several years of research, and is now recognised as the standard account of the development of crofting. He has produced, 'In the People's Cause', a selection of the writings of the Scottish and Irish land pioneer, John Murdoch, published by the Crofters' Commission to mark the centenary of the Crofters Act. He has been a journalist and broadcaster, as well as the development consultant for Rural Forum. He now lives in Skye where he is the full-time Director of the Scottish Crofters' Union.

Dr FRANK RENNIE is a graduate in geology from Aberdeen University. He 'married' into the crofting community, and has farmed a croft in Lewis for the last five years. He combines crofting, which is mainly concentrated on sheep, with work as a Scientific Officer doing general environmental and conservation work for the Nature Conservancy Council. He travels widely and writes regularly for the Aberdeen Press and Journal, and the West Highland Free Press. He takes an active part in crofting politics and is the President of the Scottish Crofters' Union.